GIBRALTAR
TRAVEL GUIDE 2025

Discover Gibraltar : your ultimate Guide to the Island wonders and Delight

JOAN RILEY

TABLE OF CONTENTS

4.0 ACCOMODATION

5.0 SHOPPING IN GIBRALTAR

6.0 FOOD AND DRINKS

10.0 PRACTICAl TIPS

11.0 CONCLUSION

WELCOME NOTE

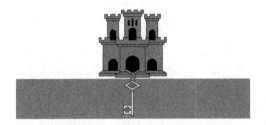

Welcome to Gibraltar!Whether you're a first-time visitor or returning to this iconic British Overseas Territory, our Gibraltar Travel Guide 2025 is here to make your journey unforgettable.

Gibraltar is a place where cultures converge, and history is ever-present, all against the backdrop of the stunning Rock of Gibraltar. You'll find yourself surrounded by rich history, vibrant culture, and some of the most breathtaking views in the Mediterranean.

In this guide, we've packed in everything you need to know to navigate Gibraltar like a local—from the best places to eat and drink, to the must-see sights, hidden gems, and insider tips that will help you make the most of your time here. Whether you're eager to explore the famous Rock, take in the panoramic views from the Skywalk, or wander the charming streets of the town center, we've got you covered.

We've also included sections on Gibraltar's unique blend of British, Spanish, and North African influences that make it such a fascinating destination. And for those of you who love to get off the beaten path, we've highlighted some lesser-known spots that are sure to surprise and delight. So grab your camera, your sense of adventure, and let's dive into everything this extraordinary destination has to offer.

We're thrilled to be your guide as you uncover the wonders of Gibraltar in 2025. Happy travels!

1.0 INTRODUCTION

1.1 Overview

Gibraltar is a peninsular territory that spans just 6.7 square kilometers, yet its impact on the region and its significance on the global stage is profound. The territory is bordered by Spain to the north and is surrounded by the Mediterranean Sea to the east, south, and west. The iconic Rock of Gibraltar, a massive limestone promontory, dominates the landscape and is home to a rich array of flora and fauna, including the famous Barbary macaques, Europe's only wild monkeys.

With a population of around 34,000 residents, Gibraltar is a vibrant, multicultural community where British, Spanish, Genoese, Jewish, and North African influences coexist harmoniously. The official language is English, but Spanish is also widely spoken, reflecting the territory's proximity to Spain and its historical ties with the Iberian Peninsula.

Gibraltar's economy is diverse, with key sectors including tourism, financial services, shipping, and online gaming. The territory's unique tax regime and strategic location at the entrance to the Mediterranean have made it an attractive destination for businesses and visitors alike.

1.2 Brief History and Culture

Gibraltar's history is a Beauty woven from the threads of various empires and civilizations that have left their mark on this strategic outpost. The Rock has been inhabited since ancient times, with evidence of Neanderthal settlements dating back over 100,000 years. The Phoenicians, Carthaginians, Romans, and Moors all recognized Gibraltar's strategic importance, and each left their influence on the area.

The name "Gibraltar" derives from the Arabic "Jabal Tariq," meaning "Mount of Tariq," named after Tariq ibn Ziyad, the Moorish general who led the Muslim conquest of the Iberian Peninsula in 711 AD. The Moors held Gibraltar for over 700 years, during which time it became a key defensive stronghold.

In 1462, Gibraltar was captured by the Spanish, and it remained under Spanish control until 1704 when it was seized by an Anglo-Dutch force during the War of the Spanish Succession. The Treaty of Utrecht in 1713 formally ceded Gibraltar to Britain, a status that has been reaffirmed in subsequent treaties and by the inhabitants of Gibraltar through referenda.

The British influence is evident throughout Gibraltar, from the red post boxes and British-style pubs to the ceremonial traditions of the British military. However, the cultural landscape of Gibraltar is a melting pot, reflecting the diverse origins of its inhabitants. The territory celebrates a range of cultural events, including the Gibraltar National Day, celebrated on September

10th, which highlights the Gibraltarians' strong sense of identity and pride in their heritage.

1.3 Why Visit Gibraltar?

Gibraltar offers a unique travel experience that combines history, natural beauty, and cultural diversity. Visitors are drawn to the territory for various reasons, each discovering their own piece of Gibraltar's charm.

1. A Gateway Between Continents: Gibraltar's location at the meeting point of Europe and Africa makes it a fascinating place to explore. From the top of the Rock, you can see the coast of Morocco on a clear day, reminding you that you are standing at the crossroads of two continents.

2. Rich History

For history enthusiasts, Gibraltar is a treasure trove. The Rock itself is dotted with historical sites, from the ancient Moorish Castle to the Great Siege Tunnels, carved out during the 18th century. The territory's military history is further exemplified by the Gibraltar Museum, which provides a comprehensive overview of the area's storied past.

3. Natural Beauty

Despite its small size, Gibraltar boasts an impressive array of natural attractions. The Upper Rock Nature Reserve is a haven for wildlife and offers stunning panoramic views. The St. Michael's Cave, a network of limestone caves within the Rock, is another natural wonder, famous for its stalactites and stalagmites.

4. Cultural Fusion: Gibraltar's multicultural society is a unique blend of influences from the UK, Spain, and beyond. This fusion is evident in the territory's cuisine, festivals, and daily life. Whether you're enjoying fish and chips at a British pub or sampling tapas at a Spanish restaurant, the cultural

diversity of Gibraltar enriches your experience.

5. Shopping and Leisure

Gibraltar is also a shopper's paradise, known for its duty-free shopping. Main Street, the bustling heart of Gibraltar's commercial district, offers a wide range of shops, from high-end boutiques to traditional British stores. Beyond shopping, visitors can enjoy a variety of leisure activities, including dolphin-watching tours in the Bay of Gibraltar or relaxing on one of the territory's beaches.

Gibraltar is more than just a rock; it is a destination that offers a unique blend of history, culture, and natural beauty. Whether you're a history buff, a nature lover, or simply seeking a place that offers something different, Gibraltar is a destination worth exploring.

2.0 PLANNING YOUR TRIP

2.1 Best Time to Visit

Gibraltar enjoys a Mediterranean climate, making it a year-round destination. However, the best time to visit depends on your preferences and the activities you want to enjoy:

1. Spring (March to May)

Spring is an ideal time to visit Gibraltar, as temperatures are mild and comfortable, ranging from 15°C to 22°C (59°F to 72°F). The landscape is lush, and it's a great time for outdoor activities like hiking, bird watching, and exploring the natural reserves.

2. Summer (June to August)

Summers in Gibraltar are hot, with temperatures often reaching up to 30°C (86°F) or higher. This is peak tourist season, especially for beachgoers and those interested in water activities. The vibrant atmosphere and festivals, like the Gibraltar Music Festival, make it an exciting time to visit, though it can be crowded.

3. Autumn (September to November)

Autumn offers pleasant temperatures similar to spring, with fewer tourists. It's a great time to explore Gibraltar's historical sites, enjoy the beaches, and partake in local events. September is especially beautiful as the summer heat begins to wane.

4. Winter (December to February)

Winters are mild, with temperatures rarely dropping below 10°C (50°F). This is the quietest season, ideal for travelers who prefer a more peaceful experience. While some attractions may have reduced hours, winter is perfect for exploring the Rock of Gibraltar and other historical sites without the crowds.

2.2 Visa and Entry Requirements

Gibraltar is a British Overseas Territory, so entry requirements vary depending on your nationality:

1. EU/EEA and Swiss Citizens: If you're an EU, EEA, or Swiss citizen, you don't need a visa to enter Gibraltar. A valid passport or national identity card is sufficient for stays up to 90 days.

2. UK Citizens: UK citizens can enter Gibraltar with just a passport, no visa is required.

Other Nationalities: Travelers from countries outside the EU/EEA or Switzerland may require a visa to enter Gibraltar. If you need a visa to enter the UK, you'll generally need one for Gibraltar as well. It's advisable to check the latest requirements through your local British Embassy or consulate.

3. Entry Points: The main entry point is via the land border with Spain at La Línea de la Concepción. There are also ferry services from Morocco and flights from the UK and other European cities to Gibraltar International Airport.

4. Customs Regulations: Gibraltar has its own customs regulations. Be mindful of duty-free allowances, especially if you're planning to purchase alcohol, tobacco, or luxury goods.

2.3 Currency and Banking

Gibraltar uses the Gibraltar Pound (GIP), which is on par with the British Pound Sterling (GBP). Here's what you need to know:

1. Currency

The Gibraltar Pound (GIP) is the local currency, but British Pound Sterling (GBP) is also widely accepted. GIP banknotes and coins are unique to Gibraltar, but they are not accepted in the UK. Make sure to exchange any leftover GIP before leaving.

2. ATMs and Credit Cards

ATMs are readily available, and most will dispense both GIP and GBP. Credit and debit cards are widely accepted in hotels, restaurants, and shops. However, it's always a good idea to carry some cash, especially for small purchases or in more remote areas.

3. Banking Hours: Banks in Gibraltar typically operate from 9:00 AM to 4:30 PM, Monday to Friday. Some banks may close for a lunch break, so it's advisable to plan accordingly if you need to visit.

4. Currency Exchange: Currency exchange services are available at banks, exchange bureaus, and some hotels. The exchange rates are generally favorable, but it's always good to shop around for the best rates.

2.4 Health and Safety Tips

Gibraltar is a safe destination with a well-developed healthcare system, but it's still important to be prepared:

1. Healthcare

Gibraltar has a modern healthcare system with a hospital and several clinics. If you're a UK citizen, you can access healthcare in Gibraltar under the same terms as in the

UK, so it's wise to carry your UK Global Health Insurance Card (GHIC). Non-UK citizens should ensure they have adequate travel insurance that covers healthcare.

2. Vaccinations

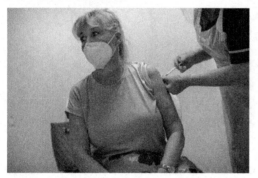

There are no mandatory vaccinations required for Gibraltar. However, it's recommended to be up-to-date with routine vaccines, including measles, mumps, rubella (MMR), diphtheria, tetanus, and influenza.

3. Sun Protection

The sun in Gibraltar can be intense, especially during the summer. Always wear sunscreen, a hat, and sunglasses to protect yourself from sunburn and heat-related illnesses. Staying hydrated is crucial, especially when exploring outdoor attractions.

4. Wildlife Caution

The Barbary macaques, Gibraltar's famous residents, are wild animals and can be unpredictable. While they're generally not dangerous, they can become aggressive if provoked or if they see food. Avoid feeding them and keep a safe distance.

5. Emergency Services: In case of an emergency, dial 112 or 999 for police, fire, or medical assistance. English is widely spoken, so you should have no trouble communicating with emergency personnel.

2.5 Packing and Essentials

Packing smartly for your trip to Gibraltar will ensure you're prepared for all the adventures that await:

1. Clothing

Spring/Autumn: Pack layers, including light sweaters or jackets for cooler evenings. Comfortable walking shoes are a must for exploring the city and nature reserves.

Summer: Light, breathable clothing is essential, along with swimwear for the beach. A sunhat, sunglasses, and sunscreen are also crucial.

Winter: Mild winters mean you'll need a light jacket, but heavy winter gear isn't necessary. Rain is possible, so a compact umbrella or rain jacket might come in handy. Travel Documents: Ensure your passport is valid for the duration of your stay. If you need a visa, have it sorted well in advance. Keep copies of important documents like your passport, visa, and travel insurance policy.

2. Electronics: Gibraltar uses the same type of electrical outlets as the UK (Type G), so if you're coming from outside the UK, you'll need an adapter. Don't forget your phone charger, and consider bringing a power bank for days out.

3. Essentials: A small first aid kit with basic medications (pain relievers, anti-diarrheal, motion sickness tablets) can be helpful. Don't forget any prescription medications you may need, along with a copy of the prescription.

4. Guidebook/Map: While Gibraltar is small and easy to navigate, a good guidebook or map can enhance your experience by providing insights into the sites you're visiting.

By carefully planning your trip to Gibraltar, you can ensure a hassle-free experience, allowing you to focus on soaking in the rich history, natural beauty, and vibrant culture of this unique destination.

3.0 TRANSPORTOTION

3.1 Getting to Gibraltar

1. By Air

Gibraltar International Airport (GIB) is the main point of entry for travelers flying into the region. The airport, located just 500 meters from Gibraltar's city center, is one of the most unique airports globally, with its runway intersecting the main road that connects Gibraltar to Spain. When a plane is about to land or take off, barriers close the road, offering a spectacle that fascinates visitors.

Flights to Gibraltar are available from major cities in the United Kingdom, including

London, Manchester, and Bristol. Seasonal flights from other European cities may also be available. For those traveling from outside Europe, connecting through UK airports is the most straightforward option.

2. By Land

Most visitors arrive in Gibraltar by road, crossing the border from Spain at La Línea de la Concepción. The border crossing is relatively straightforward, though it can become busy during peak times, especially in the summer months. Visitors can enter Gibraltar by car, bus, or on foot.

By Car

Driving into Gibraltar is simple, though parking can be challenging, especially in the city center. Visitors are advised to park in La Línea and walk across the border, taking advantage of Gibraltar's excellent public transportation system or taxis to get around.

By Bus

Several bus services operate between major Spanish cities and the border at La Línea. These include routes from Malaga, Seville, and Madrid. From La Línea, it's just a short walk across the border into Gibraltar.

3. By Sea

Gibraltar's deep-water port is a popular stop for cruise ships traveling through the Mediterranean. The port is located near the city center, making it easy for cruise passengers to disembark and explore Gibraltar's attractions. While regular passenger ferry services between Gibraltar and other ports are limited, private yachts and boats frequently dock here, taking advantage of the modern marina facilities.

4. By Rail

There is no direct rail connection to Gibraltar. However, travelers can take a train to Algeciras, a major railway hub in Spain, and then catch a bus or taxi to La Línea, where they can cross the border on foot.

3.2 Getting Around Gibraltar

1. By Foot:
Gibraltar is compact, and much of it is easily explored on foot. The city center, known as Main Street, is pedestrian-friendly, with shops, restaurants, and landmarks within easy walking distance of each other. Walking is the best way to experience the

narrow streets and discover hidden gems in the city. The area around the Rock of Gibraltar, however, is steep, so be prepared for some uphill walking if you choose to explore this iconic site on foot.

2. By Taxi

Taxis are readily available throughout Gibraltar and are a convenient way to reach specific destinations, especially if you're traveling with luggage or want to visit more remote areas like the Great Siege Tunnels or St. Michael's Cave. Taxis can be hailed on the street, found at designated ranks, or booked in advance. Many taxi drivers also offer guided tours of Gibraltar, which can be a comfortable and informative way to see the highlights.

3. By Bicycle

Cycling in Gibraltar is becoming increasingly popular, with several bike rental shops available. The compact size of the territory makes it ideal for cycling, though the steep roads up the Rock can be challenging. A bicycle is a great way to explore the flatter areas of Gibraltar, such as the east side beaches or the historic district.

4. By Cable Car

The Gibraltar Cable Car is a must-try for visitors, offering a scenic and convenient way to reach the top of the Rock of Gibraltar. The ride provides stunning views of the city, the Mediterranean Sea, and on clear days, the African coast. The upper station of the cable car gives access to some of Gibraltar's top attractions, including the famous Barbary macaques and the nature reserve.

About $17 00. Return trip

5. By Scooter or Moped

For those who want a bit more freedom but
don't want to deal with the challenges of
driving a car, renting a scooter or moped
can be a fun alternative. It allows you to
navigate Gibraltar's narrow streets easily
and find parking more readily than a car.

6. By Boat

For a unique perspective of Gibraltar, consider taking a boat tour. Various operators offer dolphin-watching tours in the Bay of Gibraltar, giving you the chance to see these playful creatures up close. Some tours also offer views of the Rock and the surrounding coastline from the water, providing a different vantage point of this historic landmark.

whether you choose to walk, take public transport, or use a more novel mode of transport like the cable car, getting around Gibraltar is relatively straightforward and offers plenty of options for all types of travelers.

4.0 ACCOMODATION

4.1 Luxury Hotels

For those who seek the finer things in life, Gibraltar offers a selection of luxury hotels that combine elegance, comfort, and top-notch service. These hotels often provide breathtaking views of the Mediterranean Sea, the iconic Rock of Gibraltar, and even the coast of Africa on clear days. Here are some top choices:

1. The Rock Hotel

A symbol of Gibraltar's colonial past, The Rock Hotel is one of the most iconic and historic hotels on the peninsula. Perched on the side of the Rock, this hotel offers panoramic views of the Bay of Gibraltar and the African coast. The rooms are elegantly furnished, blending traditional charm with modern amenities. The hotel features a beautiful garden, a swimming pool with sea views, and a restaurant serving Mediterranean cuisine. Staying here feels like stepping back in time while enjoying all the comforts of the modern world.

2. Sunborn Gibraltar

A floating luxury hotel moored in Ocean Village, Sunborn Gibraltar is a unique and opulent option for travelers. This superyacht hotel offers spacious, beautifully appointed rooms with floor-to-ceiling windows providing stunning sea views. The Sunborn boasts several fine dining options, a luxurious spa, and a rooftop pool with panoramic views of the Mediterranean. It's perfect for those who want to experience the glamour of staying on a luxury yacht without leaving the dock.

3. The Caleta Hotel

This Place HAS BEEN Demolished ? — 2022. THERE SHOULD BE A New Hotel in its Place.

Located on the eastern side of Gibraltar, The Caleta Hotel offers a tranquil escape from the bustling city center. This luxury hotel is set on the shores of Catalan Bay, providing guests with a peaceful beachside retreat. The Caleta combines modern amenities with Mediterranean charm, featuring a spa, a fitness center, and multiple dining options, including a renowned seafood restaurant. The rooms are spacious, many with balconies overlooking the sea, offering a serene environment to unwind.

4.2 Budget-Friendly Options

Travelers on a budget need not worry, as Gibraltar has plenty of affordable accommodation options that do not compromise on comfort or convenience. These options are ideal for those looking to explore Gibraltar without breaking the bank.

1. The Bristol Hotel

One of Gibraltar's oldest hotels, The Bristol offers a budget-friendly stay with a central location. It's within walking distance of Main Street, the Gibraltar Museum, and many of the city's attractions. The hotel features simple, clean rooms, a small swimming pool, and a continental breakfast. It's a great option for travelers who want to be in the heart of Gibraltar without spending too much.

2. The Cannon Hotel

Situated near Casemates Square, The Cannon Hotel is a modest, budget-friendly option perfect for travelers who prioritize location and value. The rooms are basic but comfortable, offering all the essentials for a pleasant stay. The hotel has a small restaurant and bar, making it convenient for guests to grab a meal or a drink before heading out to explore Gibraltar's many attractions.

3. Emile Youth Hostel

For those seeking even more affordable accommodation, Emile Youth Hostel is a great choice. Located in the city center, this hostel offers dormitory-style rooms as well as private rooms for those who prefer more privacy. The atmosphere is friendly and welcoming, making it easy to meet fellow travelers. The hostel provides basic amenities, including free Wi-Fi, a communal kitchen, and a shared lounge area.

4.3 Unique Stays

For travelers looking for something out of the ordinary, Gibraltar has some unique accommodations that offer a memorable experience. These options allow you to stay in places that reflect the rich history, culture, and natural beauty of Gibraltar.

1. Camp Bay Cabins

Located in the quieter Camp Bay area, these rustic cabins offer a unique stay right by the sea. The cabins are simple but cozy, providing a close-to-nature experience that's perfect for those who love the outdoors. Wake up to the sound of waves, enjoy your morning coffee with a sea view, and spend your day exploring the nearby beaches or taking a dip in the natural swimming pools. It's a great way to experience Gibraltar's coastal beauty in a more intimate setting.

2. Stay on a Sailboat

For a truly unique experience, consider renting a sailboat for your stay. Moored in one of Gibraltar's marinas, these boats offer a cozy and adventurous place to sleep with all the comforts of home. You can enjoy the gentle rocking of the boat at night and wake up to stunning views of the marina and the Rock of Gibraltar. It's an ideal option for those who love the sea and want a taste of the maritime lifestyle.

The King's Bastion Leisure Centre Apartments: For a stay that combines history with modern comfort, consider renting an apartment at the King's Bastion.

Once a military fortress, the King's Bastion has been transformed into a leisure center with various amenities, including cinemas, ice skating, and a bowling alley. The apartments here are stylishly furnished, offering a unique blend of old-world charm and contemporary living. Staying here allows you to experience a piece of Gibraltar's history while enjoying modern conveniences.

Whether you're indulging in luxury, keeping an eye on your budget, or seeking a unique experience, Gibraltar's accommodation options are as diverse as its history and culture. No matter where you choose to stay, you'll be perfectly positioned to explore the many wonders that this remarkable destination has to offer.

5.0 SHOPPING IN GIBRALTAR

5.1 Main Street Shopping

Main Street is the heart of Gibraltar's shopping district, stretching from Casemates Square to the Governor's Residence. This bustling street is lined with a mix of international brands, local boutiques, and duty-free shops, making it a popular spot for both tourists and locals. The absence of VAT (Value Added Tax) in Gibraltar adds to the appeal, allowing shoppers to enjoy significant savings on a range of products.

As you stroll down Main Street, you'll find an array of shops offering everything from designer clothing and jewelry to electronics and cosmetics. International brands such as Marks & Spencer, Tommy Hilfiger, and Swarovski sit alongside local retailers, providing a diverse shopping experience. Many stores also offer British products, giving visitors a taste of home away from home.

In addition to retail shops, Main Street is home to a variety of cafes and restaurants where you can take a break and enjoy a meal or a coffee. The street itself is a blend of old and new, with historic buildings housing modern shops, creating a unique atmosphere that adds to the charm of shopping in Gibraltar.

5.2 Local Market: Fresh Produce and Artisan

For those looking to experience a more authentic side of Gibraltar, the local markets are a must-visit. The Grand Casemates Market, located near the entrance to Main Street, is a vibrant spot where you can find a variety of fresh produce, meats, and local delicacies. The market is popular with locals and offers a glimpse into the daily life of Gibraltarians.

Here, you can browse stalls filled with fresh fruits, vegetables, and seafood, much of it sourced from nearby Spain and the Mediterranean. The market is also a great place to pick up traditional Gibraltarian foods, such as calentita (a chickpea flour flatbread) and torta de acelga (a savory chard pie). Whether you're planning a picnic or simply want to sample some local flavors, the market offers a wide selection of fresh ingredients.

In addition to food, the market also features stalls selling artisan goods, including handmade jewelry, ceramics, and textiles. These products are often crafted by local artisans, making them unique souvenirs that reflect the culture and craftsmanship of Gibraltar. The market is a lively spot, particularly on weekends, when it becomes a hub of activity with locals and tourists alike.

5.3 Gibraltar Crystal

Gibraltar Crystal is one of the most renowned local products, offering beautifully crafted glassware that makes for a perfect souvenir or gift. The Gibraltar Crystal factory, located at the entrance to Casemates Square, is a popular destination for visitors interested in seeing the art of glassblowing up close.

At the factory, skilled artisans demonstrate traditional glassblowing techniques, transforming molten glass into intricate vases, bowls, and figurines. The process is fascinating to watch, and visitors can even try their hand at blowing their own piece of glass under the guidance of a master craftsman.

The factory also has a showroom where you can purchase a wide range of Gibraltar Crystal products, from elegant wine glasses to decorative ornaments. Each piece is unique, with designs often inspired by the natural beauty of Gibraltar, such as the Rock of Gibraltar or the surrounding sea. These items make for a special memento of your trip, combining artistry with local heritage.

5.4 Souvenirs and Local Products

No trip to Gibraltar is complete without picking up a few souvenirs to remember your visit. In addition to the Gibraltar Crystal, there are plenty of other local products and keepsakes that make for great gifts or personal treasures.

One popular souvenir is the miniature replica of the Rock of Gibraltar, a symbol of strength and endurance. These replicas come in various sizes and materials, from polished stone to hand-painted ceramic. They serve as a reminder of the iconic landmark that dominates Gibraltar's skyline.

Another unique product is Gibraltar's own brand of gin, which has gained a reputation for its quality and distinct flavor. The gin is crafted using locally sourced botanicals, including juniper berries found on the Rock itself. A bottle of Gibraltar gin makes for a sophisticated gift and a taste of the Mediterranean to take home.

Gibraltar is also known for its vibrant arts and crafts scene, with many local artisans creating handmade jewelry, pottery, and textiles. These items often incorporate motifs inspired by Gibraltar's rich history and natural surroundings, making them a meaningful and authentic souvenir.

For those interested in fashion, Gibraltar offers a range of locally designed clothing and accessories. Many shops on Main Street carry unique pieces that blend contemporary styles with Mediterranean influences. Whether it's a handmade leather bag or a stylish scarf, these items are both fashionable and representative of Gibraltar's cultural fusion.

Overall, shopping in Gibraltar is more than just a retail experience; it's an opportunity to explore the local culture, discover unique products, and take home a piece of this fascinating destination. From the bustling Main Street to the artisanal markets, Gibraltar offers a diverse and enjoyable shopping experience for every visitor.

6.0 FOOD AND DRINKS

6.1 Traditional Gibraltarian Cuisine

Gibraltarian cuisine is a vibrant fusion of Mediterranean, British, and Moorish influences, reflecting the region's rich cultural tapestry. Traditional dishes often incorporate fresh seafood, hearty stews, and a variety of spices.

One of the most iconic dishes is Calentita, a simple yet flavorful chickpea flour pancake. Often served as a snack or appetizer, it's a staple in Gibraltarian households and a must-try for visitors. Another popular dish is Panissa, which is similar to Calentita but is thicker and often served in fried slices, making it a deliciously crispy treat.

Rosto is another beloved Gibraltarian dish, consisting of macaroni cooked with beef or chicken, carrots, and a rich tomato sauce. This hearty pasta dish, with its comforting flavors, is a favorite among locals and visitors alike.

Gibraltar's love for seafood is evident in dishes like Bacalao, a salted cod dish that's often served with potatoes and onions. The use of salted fish harks back to times when preserving food was essential, and it remains a cherished part of the culinary heritage.

6.2 Top Restaurants

Gibraltar boasts an impressive array of dining establishments, ranging from high-end restaurants to cozy local eateries.

Whether you're seeking a fine dining experience or a casual meal, the Rock has plenty to offer.

1. The Lounge Gastro Bar

Located in Ocean Village, this trendy restaurant offers a modern twist on traditional Mediterranean dishes. The Lounge is known for its fresh seafood, including grilled octopus and seabass, and a selection of tapas that pair perfectly with their extensive wine list.

2. La Mamela

Favorite among locals, La Mamela is located in the historic Catalan Bay area. This seaside restaurant specializes in seafood, with dishes like Fideuà, a noodle-based paella, and grilled red prawns. The stunning views of the bay add to the dining experience.

3. The Rock Hotel Restaurant

For a touch of elegance, the restaurant at The Rock Hotel offers a refined dining experience with breathtaking views of the Bay of Gibraltar. The menu features a blend of British and Mediterranean cuisines, with highlights including roast lamb, fish and chips, and classic British desserts like sticky toffee pudding.

4. Nunos Italian Restaurant

Located within the Caleta Hotel, Nunos offers a taste of Italy with a focus on fresh, high-quality ingredients. Their homemade pasta dishes and wood-fired pizzas are particularly popular, and the sea views from the terrace are a delightful bonus.

6.3 Local Delicacies to Try

While exploring Gibraltar, make sure to sample some of the local delicacies that showcase the region's culinary diversity.

1. Torta de Acelgas

This savory pie, made with Swiss chard, pine nuts, raisins, and eggs, is a testament to Gibraltar's Mediterranean influences. The sweet and savory combination is unique and utterly delicious.

2. Manteca Colorá

A rich, spiced pork spread, Manteca Colorá is often served with bread or as a filling for sandwiches. It's a delicacy that reflects the Andalusian influence on Gibraltarian cuisine.

3. Pastelitos

These sweet pastries, filled with almonds, honey, and spices, are a nod to Gibraltar's Moorish past. Often enjoyed with a cup of coffee or tea, they're a perfect treat to indulge in.

4. Polvorones

A traditional Spanish shortbread cookie that's popular in Gibraltar, especially during the Christmas season. Made with flour, sugar, and almonds, these crumbly cookies are a delightful sweet snack.

5. Bollo de Hornasso

A type of savory bread filled with hard-boiled eggs and chorizo, Bollo de Hornasso is a unique and flavorful treat that's often enjoyed during festive occasions.

6.4 Street Food and Markets

Gibraltar's street food scene is a delightful blend of quick bites and traditional flavors, offering an authentic taste of the local culture. The markets and street vendors are where you can truly immerse yourself in the everyday culinary life of Gibraltar.

1. Casemates Square

The heart of Gibraltar's social life, Casemates Square is home to various food stalls and small eateries offering a range of quick bites. Here, you can find anything from freshly made sandwiches to traditional Gibraltarian snacks like Calentita and Panissa. The lively atmosphere makes it a great spot to grab a bite and people-watch.

2. Gibraltar Central Market

This historic market, located on Fish Market Road, is where you'll find the freshest local produce, meats, and seafood. While it's primarily a place to shop for ingredients, there are also small vendors selling prepared foods. It's the perfect place to try a variety of local delicacies in one visit.

3. Rosia Bay Fish Stall

For seafood lovers, the fish stall at Rosia Bay is a hidden gem. Freshly caught fish is prepared on the spot, offering an authentic and delicious experience. From grilled sardines to fried calamari, the flavors here are fresh and vibrant.

4. Pop-up Food Stalls

Throughout the year, Gibraltar hosts various events and festivals where pop-up food stalls offer a wide range of street food. These events are a fantastic opportunity to sample different cuisines, from British classics like fish and chips to Spanish tapas and North African-inspired dishes.

Gibraltar's food and drink scene is as diverse as its history, offering a blend of traditional and contemporary flavors that cater to all tastes. Whether dining in a high-end restaurant or grabbing a snack from a street vendor, the culinary delights of Gibraltar are sure to leave a lasting impression.

7.0 EXPLORING

7.1 Iconic Landmarks

1. The Rock of Gibraltar

Undoubtedly, the most iconic feature of Gibraltar is the Rock of Gibraltar. Standing at 426 meters, this limestone ridge dominates the landscape and is visible from miles around. The Rock is not just a natural wonder; it's a symbol of the territory's strategic importance throughout history. Visitors can take the cable car up to the top of the Rock, where they'll be greeted with breathtaking panoramic views of the Mediterranean, the Atlantic, and the distant mountains of Morocco. The Upper Rock Nature Reserve, located here, is home to the famous Barbary macaques, the only wild monkey population in Europe. Legends say that as long as these macaques remain, so too will British rule over Gibraltar.

2. The Great Siege Tunnels

The Great Siege Tunnels are another must-see landmark. These extensive tunnels were carved out of the Rock by the British during the Great Siege of Gibraltar in the late 18th century. The tunnels were originally intended to house cannons and serve as defense mechanisms against the combined Spanish and French forces.

Today, they are open to the public and provide a fascinating insight into the military history of Gibraltar. Walking through the tunnels, you'll see exhibits and artifacts that tell the story of the Great Siege and the role these tunnels played in the British defense.

3. Europa Point

Europa Point, the southernmost point of Gibraltar, is a place of profound geographical and historical significance. From here, you can look out over the Strait of Gibraltar and see Africa across the water. The area is home to several important landmarks, including the Trinity Lighthouse, which has been guiding ships safely through the strait since 1841. Also located at Europa Point is the Ibrahim-al-Ibrahim Mosque, a gift from King Fahd of Saudi Arabia, and the Shrine of Our Lady of Europe, highlighting Gibraltar's rich cultural and religious diversity.

7.2 Museums and Galleries

1. The Gibraltar National Museum

For those interested in delving into Gibraltar's history and culture, the Gibraltar National Museum is an essential stop. Founded in 1930, the museum is located in a building that dates back to 1726. Inside, you'll find exhibits that span Gibraltar's history from the prehistoric Neanderthals to the modern day. Highlights include the remains of a 14th-century Moorish bathhouse, the model of Gibraltar as it appeared in 1865, and exhibits on the Great Siege and World War II. The museum also houses an extensive natural history collection, showcasing the unique flora and fauna of the region.

2. The Gibraltar Art Gallery

Art enthusiasts will appreciate a visit to the Gibraltar Art Gallery, which celebrates the works of local and international artists. The gallery is known for its diverse collection of paintings, sculptures, and mixed-media works that reflect Gibraltar's unique position at the crossroads of cultures. Temporary exhibitions often feature contemporary works that explore themes relevant to Gibraltar's history, identity, and its role as a melting pot of cultures.

3. The Military Heritage Centre

Gibraltar's military history is further explored at the Military Heritage Centre, located within the Princess Caroline's Battery. This museum provides a detailed look at Gibraltar's military past, with exhibits covering everything from the early days of the British garrison to the role of Gibraltar in World War II. Visitors can see artifacts such as weapons, uniforms, and documents that illustrate the strategic importance of Gibraltar over the centuries.

7.3 Parks and Gardens

1. The Alameda Botanical Gardens

Amidst the hustle and bustle of Gibraltar, the Alameda Botanical Gardens offer a peaceful retreat. Established in 1816, these gardens were originally created as a place of relaxation for British soldiers stationed in Gibraltar. Today, they are open to the public and serve as a beautiful green space where locals and visitors can enjoy a leisurely stroll. The gardens are home to a wide variety of plants, both native and exotic, and are particularly noted for their collection of succulents and cacti. The Alameda also plays host to the Gibraltar Botanic Gardens Wildlife Park, where visitors can see animals native to Gibraltar and the surrounding region.

2. The Commonwealth Park

For a more modern green space, the Commonwealth Park is a must-visit. Opened in 2014, this park is located in the heart of Gibraltar and offers a tranquil environment with its expansive lawns, water features, and carefully landscaped gardens.

The park is a popular spot for picnics, outdoor events, and family outings. It also provides a stunning backdrop for the various sculptures and art installations that are dotted throughout the area.

3. The Upper Rock Nature Reserve

While primarily known for its wildlife and stunning views, the Upper Rock Nature Reserve is also home to several beautiful green spaces. Walking trails wind through areas of natural beauty, with Mediterranean scrub, wildflowers, and endemic plants creating a rich Beauty of colors. Visitors can explore the reserve at their own pace, taking in the breathtaking views while also enjoying the peace and tranquility of nature.

Gibraltar may be small, but it offers a wealth of experiences for those eager to explore. From its iconic landmarks like the Rock of Gibraltar and the Great Siege Tunnels to its fascinating museums, galleries, and serene parks and gardens, there is something to captivate every visitor. Whether you're a history buff, a nature lover, or simply someone looking to soak up the unique atmosphere of this remarkable place, Gibraltar promises an unforgettable journey.

8.0 OUTDOOR ADVENTURES

8.1 Hiking and Walking Trails

Gibraltar's compact size belies the wealth of hiking opportunities it offers. The iconic Rock of Gibraltar, rising to 426 meters, is home to a network of trails that provide both easy walks and more challenging hikes, all set against breathtaking backdrops.

One of the most popular hikes is the Mediterranean Steps, a steep, challenging trail that rewards hikers with panoramic views of the Mediterranean Sea, the Moroccan coastline, and the Spanish hinterlands. This trail, carved into the cliffside, takes you through rich flora and fauna, and ends at the summit of the Rock, where the views are nothing short of spectacular.

For a more leisurely walk, the Upper Rock Nature Reserve offers several trails that wind through lush vegetation, historical sites, and points of interest such as the Apes' Den, where you can encounter the famous Barbary macaques. The Governor's Lookout is another must-visit spot, offering stunning vistas over the Bay of Gibraltar and the city itself.

The Nature Lover's Walk is ideal for those interested in Gibraltar's biodiversity. This trail takes you through varied ecosystems, showcasing the area's unique plants and wildlife. The Europa Point, the southernmost point of Gibraltar, also offers an easier walk, allowing you to enjoy the views of the Strait of Gibraltar, the African coast, and the lighthouse.

8.2 Bird Watching

Gibraltar is a paradise for bird watchers, especially during the spring and autumn migration seasons. The Rock's strategic position at the crossroads of Europe and Africa makes it a crucial stopover for thousands of migrating birds. As they journey between the continents, these birds use the updrafts created by Gibraltar's cliffs to gain height before crossing the Strait of Gibraltar.

The Gibraltar Ornithological & Natural History Society (GONHS) operates several bird observatories on the Rock, providing excellent vantage points for spotting a wide range of species. Raptors are particularly abundant, with species such as the Booted Eagle, Short-toed Eagle, and Honey Buzzard frequently seen soaring over the Rock. The Jew's Gate Observatory is one of the best locations to observe these magnificent birds in flight.

In addition to raptors, Gibraltar is also home to a variety of resident and migratory species, including warblers, swifts, and the colorful Bee-eater. The Lower Slopes of the Rock are particularly rich in birdlife, with scrubland and woodland providing habitat for many smaller species.

Whether you're an experienced birder or a casual nature enthusiast, the sight of thousands of birds crossing the narrow strait is an unforgettable experience, showcasing nature's incredible spectacle in one of the world's most significant migratory corridors.

8.3 Rock Climbing

Gibraltar's rugged limestone cliffs are a magnet for rock climbers of all levels. The Rock offers a variety of routes that cater to beginners and seasoned climbers alike, with challenges ranging from easy scrambles to technically demanding ascents.

One of the most popular climbing areas is The Great North Face of the Rock, which presents a variety of routes that offer stunning views over the town and bay. The Douglas Path also provides excellent climbing opportunities, with routes that take you along the exposed ridges of the Rock, offering both excitement and breathtaking scenery.

For those new to rock climbing, several local guides and companies offer climbing tours and instruction, ensuring a safe and enjoyable experience. These guided climbs often include routes that allow climbers to explore hidden corners of the Rock, including tunnels and caves that are otherwise inaccessible.

The limestone cliffs are not only challenging but also provide climbers with a sense of history, as many routes pass by remnants of

Gibraltar's military past, such as gun emplacements and fortifications.

8.4 Water Sports

Surrounded by the waters of the Mediterranean Sea and the Atlantic Ocean, Gibraltar is a fantastic destination for water sports enthusiasts. The meeting of these two bodies of water creates unique conditions that are perfect for a range of activities.

Kayaking is one of the most popular water sports in Gibraltar. Exploring the coastline by kayak allows you to discover hidden coves, sea caves, and beaches that are inaccessible by land. The waters around the Rock are generally calm, making kayaking suitable for all levels. Guided tours are available, offering insights into the area's history and natural features as you paddle along.

Stand-up Paddleboarding (SUP) is another excellent way to explore Gibraltar's waters. The relatively calm seas make it an ideal location for both beginners and experienced paddleboarders. SUP tours often take you along the coast, offering unique views of the Rock and the chance to spot marine wildlife such as dolphins.

For the more adventurous, scuba diving in Gibraltar offers an underwater world rich in marine life and historical wrecks. The area is home to several dive sites, including the wreck of the S.S. Rosslyn, a steamer that sank in 1916, and the Seven Sisters, a group of underwater pinnacles teeming with life. Whether you're a novice or an experienced diver, Gibraltar's waters offer fascinating dives that reveal the hidden treasures of the sea.

Sailing is also a popular activity, with the Strait of Gibraltar offering some of the best sailing conditions in the region. The constant breeze and challenging currents provide an exhilarating experience for sailors. Several companies offer sailing charters, allowing you to explore the waters around Gibraltar, or even venture across the strait to Morocco or Spain.

Whether you're exploring the underwater world, paddling along the coast, or sailing the strait, Gibraltar's diverse marine environment offers something for every water sports enthusiast, making it a key part of any outdoor adventure in this unique destination.

9.0 ENTERTAINMENT AND NIGHT LIFE

9.1 Night Clubs and Bars

Gibraltar may be small, but it packs a punch when it comes to nightlife, particularly in its nightclubs and bars. The area around Casemates Square and Ocean Village Marina is a hotspot for evening revelry, with many establishments staying open late into the night.

Casemates Square is the heart of Gibraltar's nightlife. As the sun sets, the square's many bars and pubs come alive with locals and tourists alike. Here, you'll find a mix of traditional British pubs like The Clipper and more modern cocktail bars. The atmosphere is lively yet relaxed, making it an ideal spot for a night of bar hopping. Many bars feature outdoor seating, perfect for enjoying Gibraltar's warm evenings with a pint of ale or a classic gin and tonic.

For those looking to dance the night away, Ocean Village Marina is the place to be. This area is home to some of Gibraltar's trendiest nightclubs, where international DJs spin tracks ranging from house and techno to commercial hits. Clubs like Dusk and La Sala are known for their stylish interiors, energetic atmospheres, and panoramic views of the marina, adding a touch of glamour to your night out. La Sala in particular is a favorite for those who want to start the evening with a sophisticated dinner before transitioning to the dance floor.

Irish Town, another key area, is dotted with pubs and bars that offer a more laid-back vibe. Establishments like The Horseshoe and The Lord Nelson are popular for their extensive drink menus, including craft beers and specialty cocktails, along with live sports broadcasts and friendly atmospheres.

9.2 Live Music Venues

Gibraltar's live music scene is diverse, catering to a wide range of tastes. From intimate acoustic performances to full-blown rock concerts, the territory has plenty of venues that showcase local talent as well as international acts.

One of the top spots for live music is the Sunborn Gibraltar Yacht Hotel in Ocean Village. This luxury hotel hosts regular live music nights, where you can enjoy performances by local bands and solo artists in a chic, upscale setting. Genres range from jazz and blues to pop and rock, ensuring there's something for everyone.

For a more traditional experience, head to The Lord Nelson in Casemates Square, a historic pub with a reputation for its lively atmosphere and regular live music events. The venue frequently hosts local rock and blues bands, making it a popular spot for those who appreciate good music in a relaxed, unpretentious setting.

Another noteworthy venue is The Kasbar in Irish Town, known for its eclectic mix of music genres and artists. This quirky, bohemian-style bar is a favorite among the alternative crowd and often features acoustic sessions, indie bands, and even the occasional DJ set. The Kasbar's intimate atmosphere and unique décor make it a standout venue in Gibraltar's live music scene.

During the warmer months, you can also catch live performances in outdoor settings. Ocean Village often hosts live music events on the marina, where you can enjoy the tunes alongside stunning sea views and a refreshing breeze. These events are typically free and attract a diverse crowd, creating a vibrant and inclusive atmosphere.

9.3 Night Tours

For those looking to experience Gibraltar's nightlife from a different perspective, night tours offer a unique and memorable way to explore the territory after dark. These tours often focus on the history and natural beauty of Gibraltar, providing a fascinating contrast to the bustling nightlife in the town.

One of the most popular night tours is the Upper Rock Night Tour, which allows visitors to explore the famous Rock of Gibraltar under the stars. Led by knowledgeable guides, this tour takes you through the Upper Rock Nature Reserve, where you'll encounter Gibraltar's iconic Barbary macaques, explore hidden caves, and enjoy panoramic views of the city lights below. The tour often includes a visit to St.

Michael's Cave, where a sound and light show adds a magical touch to the experience.

Another intriguing option is the Ghost Walk of Gibraltar, a tour that delves into the territory's haunted history. As you wander through the narrow, winding streets of the old town, your guide will recount chilling tales of ghostly apparitions, mysterious occurrences, and the darker side of Gibraltar's past. This tour is perfect for those who enjoy a thrill and want to see a different side of the Rock.

For a more relaxed evening, consider a Sunset Cruise around Gibraltar's coastline. These cruises typically depart from Ocean Village and offer stunning views of the sun setting over the Mediterranean. Some cruises include dinner and drinks, making it a perfect way to unwind and take in the beauty of Gibraltar at dusk.

No matter how you choose to spend your evenings, Gibraltar's nightlife and entertainment options provide a rich Beauty of experiences, blending cultural exploration with lively social scenes and unforgettable adventures.

10.0 PRACTICAI TIPS

10.1 Language and Communication

Primary Language: English is the official language of Gibraltar, and it's used in all official communications, road signs, and most public services. You'll find that locals are fluent and comfortable speaking English, so communication should be straightforward.

1. Local Dialect: While English is predominant, Gibraltarians often mix English with Spanish and a local dialect known as Llanito. This mixture of languages, along with a range of accents, can be heard in casual conversation. Don't be surprised if you hear some Spanish or even a unique blend of both languages!

2. Spanish Usage: Due to Gibraltar's proximity to Spain, many residents also speak Spanish, and you'll find that some signs and menus are bilingual. Knowing a few basic Spanish phrases can be helpful, especially when interacting with locals in more informal settings or when traveling to nearby Spanish towns.

3. Mobile and Internet: Gibraltar has good mobile phone coverage, and most international networks work here. However, it's advisable to check with your provider about roaming charges. Free Wi-Fi is widely available in public places, hotels, and cafes. If you need a local SIM card, you can purchase one from various shops and kiosks throughout the area.

10.2 Photography Etiquette

Public Places: Photography is generally permitted in most public areas of Gibraltar, including landmarks, streets, and parks. However, it's always courteous to ask for permission before photographing individuals, especially in more private or sensitive situations.

Military and Government Sites: Be cautious when taking photos near military or government buildings. While many areas are open to tourists, photography restrictions may apply. Look for signs indicating no photography zones and respect these regulations.

1. Wildlife

Gibraltar is famous for its Barbary macaques, the only wild monkeys in Europe. While these animals are a popular attraction, keep a respectful distance. Avoid feeding them or attempting to handle them, as this can be dangerous and disrupt their natural behavior. Always follow guidelines provided by local authorities when interacting with wildlife.

2. Commercial Photography: If you plan to use your photos for commercial purposes, such as in publications or advertisements, you may need to obtain special permission. Contact local authorities or relevant organizations in advance to ensure compliance with any regulations.

10.3 General Emergency Contact

Emergency Services: For all emergency services, dial 112, the universal emergency number. This number connects you to police, fire, and medical services and is available 24/7.

1. Local Police: For non-emergency police assistance, you can contact the Gibraltar Police at +350 200 72500. The police station is located at Casemates Square.

2. Medical Services: In case of a medical emergency, you can go to St. Bernard's Hospital, which is the main hospital in Gibraltar. The hospital's emergency department can be reached at +350 200 72266.

3. Consular Services: If you need assistance from your home country's consulate, Gibraltar has a British Consulate at 75-77 Main Street. The consulate provides support for British nationals, including in emergencies. Contact them at +350 200 72114.

4. Fire Department: For fire emergencies, dial +350 200 73000. The fire department is trained to handle a range of incidents from small fires to more significant emergencies.

5. Embassies: Gibraltar does not have many embassies due to its small size. However, if you need consular assistance from countries other than the UK, your nearest embassy or consulate in Spain or the UK can offer support. Ensure you have the contact details of your home country's diplomatic representation before traveling.

By keeping these practical tips in mind, you can navigate Gibraltar more comfortably and ensure a smooth and enjoyable visit.

Let me know if you need further details or adjustments!

11.0 CONCLUSION

As you close the pages of this guide, it's clear that Gibraltar is much more than a mere geographical location; it is a vibrant blend of cultures, a haven of natural beauty, and a testament to enduring history. From its iconic Rock to its eclectic blend of British and Mediterranean influences, Gibraltar stands out as a unique destination that promises memorable experiences for every traveler.

The Rock of Gibraltar, with its towering presence, serves as both a literal and metaphorical anchor for this remarkable destination. Its sheer cliffs and panoramic views are not just a sight to behold but also a reminder of the strategic significance and historical richness that define Gibraltar. Whether you're scaling its heights, exploring its hidden caves, or simply marveling at the expansive vistas from its summit, the Rock remains the centerpiece of any visit, a natural wonder intertwined with human history. For the food enthusiast, Gibraltar offers a delectable journey through its culinary landscape.

From savoring traditional fish and chips at a local pub to indulging in a rich Spanish paella, the local cuisine is a celebration of the region's unique cultural melting pot. The vibrant markets and cozy eateries provide a window into the everyday life of Gibraltar's residents, offering an authentic taste of the local flavors. Moreover, Gibraltar's natural beauty extends beyond the Rock. The nearby beaches, such as Catalan Bay and Eastern Beach, offer a serene escape from the bustling city life, inviting visitors to unwind and soak up the Mediterranean sun. The surrounding natural parks and nature reserves provide ample opportunities for outdoor adventures, whether you're hiking through scenic trails or spotting local wildlife. The unique combination of sea and mountain landscapes creates an environment where relaxation and exploration go hand in hand. In reflecting on your journey through Gibraltar, it's evident that this destination offers more than just a list of attractions; it presents a rich Beauty of experiences that are deeply intertwined with its historical, cultural, and natural heritage.

As you prepare to venture beyond the pages of this guide, carry with you the memories of Gibraltar's distinct charm. Let the echoes of its history, the flavors of its cuisine, and the vibrancy of its culture continue to inspire and enrich your travels.

Whether you are a history buff, a food lover, an adventure seeker, or simply a curious traveler, Gibraltar offers a unique and multifaceted experience. It invites you to explore, to engage, and to immerse yourself in a destination that is as diverse as it is enchanting. So, as you bid farewell to this remarkable place, take with you the spirit of Gibraltar, a city that effortlessly bridges the past and the present, the familiar and the exotic, ensuring that your visit will be remembered as a truly exceptional journey.

This conclusion ties together the various aspects of Gibraltar, highlighting its unique characteristics and leaving readers with a sense of the destination's overall appeal.

Printed in Dunstable, United Kingdom